Dream Doodles

A COLORING BOOK WITH A HIDDEN PICTURE TWIST

KATHY AHRENS

DOVER PUBLICATIONS, INC.
MINEOLA, NEW YORK

This coloring book features twenty-eight intricate images designed to offer a mind-expanding experience to the advanced colorist. But there's more here than meets the eye—look closely to find the bees, butterflies, tea cups, mushrooms, and other surprising figures hidden amid the wild, swirling designs. Answers are included, and the illustrations are printed on one side of a perforated page only for easy removal and display.

Copyright
Copyright © 2015 by Dover Publications, Inc.
All rights reserved.

Bibliographical Note
Dream Doodles Coloring Book: A Coloring Book with a Hidden Picture Twist
is a new work, first published by Dover Publications, Inc., in 2015.

International Standard Book Number
ISBN-13: 978-0-486-79902-5
ISBN-10: 0-486-79902-6

Manufactured in the United States by RR Donnelley
79902606 2015
www.doverpublications.com

SOLUTIONS

page 1
Bee, Hummingbird, Sun

page 2
Mushroom, Tea Cup

page 3
Bee (2), Lotus Flower, Butterfly,
Sun, Feather, Leaf

page 4

page 5
Sun, Caterpillar

page 6
Caterpillar, Tea Cup,
Stepping Stone, Bee

page 7
Leaf, Hummingbird

page 8
Butterfly, Sun, Lady Bug

page 9
Mushroom, Sun, Hummingbird

page 10
Mushroom, Snail

page 11
Dragonfly, Hummingbird

page 12
Leaf, Sun

page 13

page 14
Frog, Dragonfly

page 15
Hummingbird, Lotus Flower, Leaf

page 16
Snail, Mushroom, Frog

page 17
Sun, Feather, Lady Bug

page 18

page 19
Dragonfly, Bee

page 20
Sun, Feather, Dove

page 21
Frog, Dragonfly, Tea Cup

page 22
Snail, Dove

page 23
Bee, Mushroom

page 24
Butterfly, Sun, Lady Bug,
Caterpillar

page 25
Butterfly, Dove, Tea Cup, Stepping
Stone, Lady Bug, Lotus Flower

page 26
Feather

page 27
Dove, Caterpillar, Stepping Stone

page 28
Lotus Flower, Snail, Sun,
Stepping Stone